THE WORLD'S CITIES

PARIS

CREDITS

Written by: Bill Garnett
Series Editor: Nicolas Wright
Series Designer: Kris Flynn
Picture Researcher: Kathy Brandt
Commissioned Photography by: Bill Garnett

Produced by Theorem Publishing Limited, 71/73 Great Portland Street,
London W1N 5DH for Marshall Cavendish Books Limited.

Published by Marshall Cavendish Books Limited, 58 Old Compton
Street, London W1V 5PA.

ISBN 0 85685 501 4

Printed in Great Britain

The following sources have contributed photographs to this title:

Daily Telegraph Colour Library/K. Kirkwood, P. Morris,
A. Woolfitt; K. W. Faulkner; French Government Tourist
Office; B. Garnett; R. Twinn; Veronese; Zefa.

Introduction to Paris

Paris, 'the city of light', is unique, It is a place of wonder and magic and almost unbelievable beauty: a city of the past, with a history that spans 2,000 years, yet a city of the future too, the largest of continental Europe and with the highest population density now of any great city in the world.

No other capital provides such a fascinating amalgam of old and new. Where else is it possible to look up from cobbled medieval streets, with houses untouched from the 12th century, to a skyline which monuments from the ancient Pharaohs share with ultra-modern cloud-reaching structures.

Paris is unique in more than a merely physical sense. For it has an atmosphere, a mystique, that is entirely its own. The city of song, the inspiration of some of the world's finest painting, its fascination is extraordinary. No other city is so revered or longed for. No other across the centuries has so drawn writers, sculptors, musicians, painters and intellectuals from every corner of the globe. They are still there today – at the boulevard cafés, taking a Pernod and watching the non-stop theatre that is the streets of Paris, with their unmatched blend of businessmen and bohemians, students and bourgeois, and the most chic and elegant women in the world.

Above all, perhaps, Paris is a city of synthesis: an intellectual and cultural centre, the meeting place of tourist and pleasure seeker, the capital of high fashion, yet equally a mighty commercial, financial and industrial nexus and the political and administrative hub of France – of which it contains one sixth of the population and reflects all that is most vital and best.

What is the essence of Paris? In the end it is indefinable: a wisp, a scent, a magic that this book will help you experience. For, blending fresh new photographs with succinct and specially written text, this sets out in informed and easy-to-follow sections just what it is that makes Paris so special. Its beauty, glamour, verve. . . as much as any book can, we have captured them for you here. So, as the French say, come in and be welcome.
'Bienvenue à Paris!'

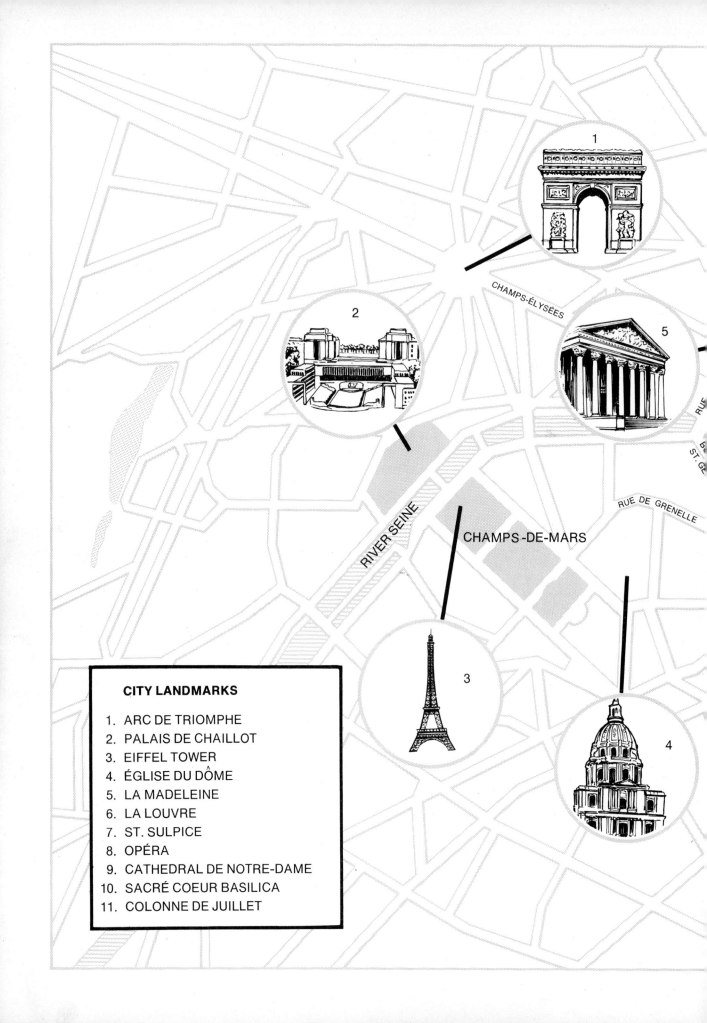

CHAMPS-ÉLYSÉES

RIVER SEINE

CHAMPS-DE-MARS

RUE DE GRENELLE

CITY LANDMARKS

1. ARC DE TRIOMPHE
2. PALAIS DE CHAILLOT
3. EIFFEL TOWER
4. ÉGLISE DU DÔME
5. LA MADELEINE
6. LA LOUVRE
7. ST. SULPICE
8. OPÉRA
9. CATHEDRAL DE NOTRE-DAME
10. SACRÉ COEUR BASILICA
11. COLONNE DE JUILLET

Setting the Scene

Paris, the capital of France, has a circumference of about 22 miles and a population of some seven million people. The city is situated in northern France, on both banks of the River Seine, 107 miles from the sea. It lies in what is known as the *Bassin de Paris,* a saucer-shaped, once-marshy area between low hills or 'buttes', the highest of which, the *Butte de Montmartre,* is only 423 feet high. Through this basin, in a great loop, the Seine flows for nearly eight miles.

The river is of incomparable importance to the city. Not only does it provide Paris with so much of her character, beauty and charm, it is largely responsible for the city's very existence. For it is here, on an island in the river, that it all began.

Paris dates back into the mists of history, but the first definite mention is made in the *Commentaries* of Julius Caesar, whose troops effortlessly conquered what was then a small village on an island in the Seine. The year was 53 BC. Little is known of that village and almost nothing remains. Marshy land extended to the hills around it and its inhabitants, a primitive Gallic tribe named the *Parisii,* lived by fishing and worshipped the river as a god. Caesar's troops named the island village *Luticia* and formed a settlement there. Although they stayed 400 years, their original name did not last. A military milestone of the year 307 is firmly engraved: 'the city of the Parisians'.

With the Seine providing a ready-made moat, the Romans were not slow to see the commanding position and strategic advantages of their island. They built a fortified camp on it and, where the church of Nôtre Dame now stands, a temple. By the 2nd century, the city had spread from the island—now called the Ile de la Cité—to the south bank and it was here the Romans erected their villas, a forum and baths.

Even in those early days, as a town of around 1,000 inhabitants, Paris was a prosperous place. A focus of highways coming from south and north, on an easily navigable river, there is no doubt that the town's geographical location influenced its future development as a capital city. The plains around it offered good travel routes and rich soils for agriculture and vineyards. A toll was probably charged on passing travellers. And money was brought in by retired officers. But the prosperity of the young city was not to last.

The might of Rome was waning, her empire near disintegration and, towards the end of the 3rd century, the Germanic tribes flowed out across the country—and put much of the city to fire and the sword. The settlement on the south (or Left) bank was destroyed and the inhabitants retreated to the island. This they fortified, using stones from their ruined homes to build a rampart. Life became increasingly precarious and, by the end of the 5th century, the hordes of Attila the Hun were marching directly on the city.

It was then that Geneviève, a young Christian and forerunner of Joan of Arc, rallied the people of Paris and saved the city from destruction—apparently, by the power of her prayers, turning aside the Huns at the last moment, so that they went on to Italy instead. As a result, Geneviève became the patron saint of Paris in her lifetime. And has remained so since.

It seems the prayers of Geneviève, however, were not so strong on a second occasion. In 508 Paris was taken by Clovis King of the Franks, whose kingdom Francia gave its name to all France. Geneviève soon converted him to Christianity and, establishing Paris as his capital, Clovis began the process of building churches and monasteries that was to continue through the centuries.

Soaring above the narrow, cobbled streets of Montmartre, the spacious white stone basilica of the Sacré-Coeur, built in the 19th century.

9

The dangers of attack were not over, though, and down the years barbarians subjected the city to periodic raids. In 845 the Norsemen looted it and in 885 they sailed up the Seine again—this time with 700 ships. The Parisians, under Count Eudis, were ready, however. They had repaired the old Roman walls and though the Norsemen laid seige to the city for ten months, Paris did not fall. And when in 911 a treaty was finally agreed with the Norse leader, Rollo, the Parisians were free from the threat of pillage. A new era was about to begin.

In 987 Hugo Capet became king of France. In doing so, he founded a new and powerful dynasty which made Paris its seat and paved the way to the city's future greatness.

In the 11th century Paris expanded onto both river banks: on the Left, schools and colleges scaled the Mont Sainte Geneviève, re-occupying the areas first settled in Roman times; on the Right, a new suburb developed as tradesmen built houses and stores.

Left: Sunset over Montmartre, once a small village and now a vital part of Paris.
Below Right: Part of the historic market of Les Halles. Dating from the 12th century, the covered part of the market alone once took up ten acres. Much of it has gone now and what is left, given over to modern redevelopment.

In the 12th century, under Louis VI and Louis VII, there were massive transformations. The city now consisted of three parts: the original Île de la Cité with its government buildings, the palace of the king and the cathedral; the Left Bank with its convents, schools and colleges—almost a city in itself with its noisy students, swarming masses of beggars, artisans and thieves; and, finally, the Right Bank inhabited by merchants and seafarers.

By this time, Paris had already developed the same basic structure that exists today: the seat of authority in the old town on the island; the academic and cultural section on the Left Bank; and the commercial and business section on the Right.

Outside the city villages appeared: Montmartre, Saint Denis and the monasteries. A frenzy of building began and it is from then that the oldest churches in Paris date: Saint Germain des Prés, Saint Julien le Pauvre and, most important of all, the incomparable Nôtre Dame.

King Philip Augustus (1180-1223) has justly been called 'The Father of Paris' because of the changes his reign brought to the city. They were many and great. The king built Les Halles as a central market; he built aquaducts to supply water, hospitals to tend the sick; repelled by the stench of the mud of the streets of the Cité, he ordered them paved. In 1190, about to go off on a crusade, and wanting to secure his city's safety, Philip decided to surround it by walls. Outside those walls, on the Right Bank, he built a formidable fortress, the Louvre, to defend the city against attack from the west.

But Paris was a hive of activity in more than just the physical sense. For it was at this time that the schools and colleges on the Left Bank federated themselves into an organization known as the University—and proclaimed self-government. They won royal privileges in 1200 and a university charter (the oldest in the West) was granted by Pope Innocent III in 1215. Throughout the 13th century the University of Paris grew and became the leading academic institution in Europe. As many as 20,000 students lived in the Left Bank colleges, forming within the city an autonomous borough, which, because Latin was its main language, became known as the Latin Quarter—as it is still known today.

It is estimated that during the 13th century the population of Paris rose to an astonishing 100,000 inhabitants. This was an age of expansion in every way. The soaring palace chapel of Sainte Chapelle was built (in only 33 months to house relics already at hand in Paris). And in 1257, under the patronage of St Louis IX, Robert de Sorbon created what was to become one of the world's most celebrated centres of culture and which still bears his name, the Sorbonne.

In the 14th and 15th centuries the growth and prosperity of Paris faded, for this was the time of the *Hundred Years War* (1339-1453).

It was a time too of the weakening of Royal authority—and, led by Etienne Marcel, a rich clothier, the merchants challenged the crown and sought reforms that amounted almost to parliamentary government. When, in 1356, the French army lost the battle of Poitiers to a much smaller English force and King John II of France was taken prisoner, Marcel led a revolt against John's son, the Dauphin Charles. Occupying his mansion as headquarters, Marcel established a form of municipal government there, but it was short-lived. Marcel himself was murdered in 1358.

When Charles duly came to the throne, to guard against further revolts, he moved the royal residence to the fortress of the Louvre which he enlarged and partly rebuilt. He also built round the Right Bank a new and larger belt of ramparts and the greatest construction of that period—the mighty fortress of La Bastille. Despite these efforts, pestilence, the effects of the war and finally capture by the English, did much to deplete the city's wealth and population.

The English held Paris for 16 years and during this time it was virtually abandoned. Joan of Arc tried to eject the invaders in 1429, but was wounded outside the Porte Sainte Honoré. Close by that site there stands a statue of her today.

Perhaps the city's lowest ebb was the year 1430—when Henry VI of England was crowned king of France in Nôtre Dame. But the occupation did not last and within five years the French had won back control of the city. Charles VII returned to the capital in 1436 and began the task of reconstruction. Things were in a sorry state for some time after, though, and a diarist of the year 1439 could note that in one month that winter 14 people between Montmartre and Saint Antoine were eaten by wolves.

Top Left: Just one of the many lovely and historic houses that border the Seine on the Ile Saint-Louis.

Above Right: The golden statue of the warrior saint Joan of Arc in the Place des Pyramides. Joan died in 1431, but people still make pilgrimages to her statue.

Bottom Right: The Petit Palais. The museum here houses a magnificent collection of modern and ancient works of art, including Eastern and Far-Eastern masterpieces.

Left: The Pavillion Richelieu – just part of the mighty edifice of the Louvre, begun as a fort in the 12th century, but today one of the greatest museums in the world.
Above: The serenity of the Tuileries gardens, named after a tile factory which once occupied the site.

The hundred years or so to 1572 were on the whole a period of peaceful growth, with the capital spilling out far beyond the walls of Charles V. During this time the Italian Renaissance made its influence felt. The city took on a new look.

The Louvre was rebuilt—transformed from a medieval fortress to a Renaissance Palace; the Tuileries gardens were laid out after the Italian manner; a new and much more splendid Hôtel de Ville was put up. The Pont Neuf was begun and the first stone quays appeared along the banks of the Seine. And on both banks too rose many elegant mansions. Everywhere the spirit of the Renaissance was expressed in the lines of the buildings, in the search for space and light.

The 17th century was the *Grand Siècle,* the great century. During these years grand and regal Paris was born. Towers gave way to Italianate domes that changed the skyline. Large, imposing buildings grew up, wide prospects, magnificent palaces. From 1600 until the Revolution in 1789 Paris was the greatest metropolis on the Continent, a centre of brilliant culture and fabulous wealth. Each new king made his contribution to the city's monuments.

Development went faster on the Right Bank than the Left and the fashionable section extended west to what is now the Place de la Concorde, while the more popular grew out to the east. Under Henri IV and Louis XIII new avenues and boulevards were laid out and lordly mansions mushroomed throughout the Marais district, replacing the old merchants' residences. Upstream from the Ile de la Cité, Louis joined two low islands. These eventually became the Ile Saint Louis.

The Louvre was expanded by each successive king and, to its west, the Tuileries Palace enlarged and joined to it. More stone bridges were built across the Seine. On the Right Bank Cardinal Richelieu built the Palais Royal. Large abbeys and convents covered much of the Left and a new college (now home of the French Academy) was established there by Cardinal Mazarin. On the Left Bank too the queen mothers had palaces built: the Luxembourg Palace for Marie de Medicis, the Val de Grace for Anne of Austria. These palaces had magnificent gardens and increasingly, throughout smart Paris, there was space and light.

The expansion of Paris continued on an even greater scale under Louis XIV though his early years were marred by the civil war named the *Fronde* (after a catapault/sling which was used by urchins in the dry moats of the city).

Incensed by already burdensome taxes the people of Paris revolted and put up barricades in the streets. The nobility sided with them against the crown. Battles were fought inside the capital itself. And intermittently, for five years the conflict went on. It ended with Louis completely victorious—and resulted in two things: an augmenting of royal power; and a widening of the gulf that already existed between the crown and people of Paris.

Indeed, so deep was Louis' distrust of his people, that he transferred the court to Versailles, building a new palace and town. Yet none of this could long halt the development of the metropolis.

Work began again on the Louvre. The Jardin des Tuileries was transformed and, in 1667, the Champs Elysées created. The old fortifications were converted and planted with trees and the first Grands Boulevards were born. Known as the 'Sun King' for the magnificence of his court and reign in which he made France the

Left: The dome of Les Invalides, a complex of buildings initiated by Louis XIV in 1671 to house and care for his wounded soldiers. In a crypt directly below the cupola is the tomb of Napoleon.
Right: The 17th century Porte Saint-Denis, one of the city's great triumphal arches.

leading nation in Europe, Louis commemorated his victories with the gates of Saint Denis and Saint Martin, the Place des Victoires and the Place Vendôme. In his reign too the great scientific institutions emerged: L'Observatoire, the Collège des Quatre Nations and the Bibliothèque Royale. Near the end of Louis' reign the Hôtel des Invalides was built—to accommodate those wounded in his wars.

But the reign of the Sun King was not all glory. Round the Louvre itself there were slums. The people had no rights and no voice. Their poverty stood out in ugly contrast to the magnificence of so many palaces and gardens. Indeed, in mid-17th century Paris it is estimated that of the population of approximately 600,000 as many as ten percent were either beggars or thieves.

Throughout the 18th century there was a flurry of building. And though Paris did not grow much in terms of population, it greatly increased in area—with many old and ugly sections razed and rebuilt with mansions.

They lined the streets of St Germain on the Left Bank and St Honoré on the Right. This was the great epoch of perspectives, of columns and fountains and grands boulevards. The bridges were cleared of houses, the ramparts broken through, the gates destroyed. The Pont de la Concorde was built to lead to (what is now) the Place de la Concorde. The Rue Royale and the Palais Bourbon were completed. The Ecole Militaire and the Théâtre de L'Odeon came into being—and Jacques-Germain Soufflot began the mighty Panthéon.

But, though the appearance of Paris was of ever-increasing splendour, the condition of many of its inhabitants was still of medieval squalor—a condition exacerbated by the so very visible wealth of the upper strata. And it brought no comfort to the poor of Paris, as they stood barefoot and threadbare with hollow bellies, to see the gilded coaches of the rich roll by.

The people of Paris were appallingly housed, overtaxed, underfed. (In the country there were still serfs.) The contrast between rich and poor, privilege and oppression could hardly have been more acute.

Perhaps what followed could have been avoided by a more perceptive, less inflexible man, but Louis XVI was a fool. With the national coffers exhausted by war in America—and further depleted by the extravagances of his queen, Marie Antoinette—he decided to call a 'States General' (a body roughly comparable to the British Parliament, but which hadn't met since 1614) with the object of raising more money by further taxation. The Assembly consisted of nobles, clergy and commons—or Third Estate. This last group decided that it alone was representative of the people and that no taxation could be levied without its consent.

Louis ordered his soldiers to disperse the Assembly. They refused to act. Pretending to agree to the Third Estate's demands, Louis then secretly called up foreign regiments of the French army. When the news of this reached the people of Paris, they rose.

On July 14th, 1789, in a great symbolic gesture they stormed the grim-looking royal prison of the Bastille, took it after three hours fighting—and destroyed it. Thereafter the insurrection spread through France: châteaux were burnt by the peasantry, their owners driven off or slain. Within a month the ancient system of the aristocratic order had gone and many leading princes and courtiers—those who were lucky—fled abroad for their lives.

Far Left: Clochards, the special vagabonds of Paris, live rough but proud, outdoors in the city. These three are taking a midday nap in the Tuileries.
Left: The Champs de Mars. In the background, the École Militaire, the UNESCO building, and above them the great Tour Montparnasse.

Now in a position of power, but without the knowledge of how to exercise it, the Assembly found itself called on to create an effective new system for a new age—but was unable to. Events followed each other relentlessly.

A shortage of bread struck Paris and on October 5th a famished people marched on the king at Versailles and forced him to return to the city. Lodged at the Tuileries, Louis dwelt there unmolested for two years and perhaps, had he kept faith with the people, might have lived out his days there as king. Foolishly, though, he attempted to slip away and raise an army—only to be ignominiously captured and returned to Paris. There on August 10th, he was attacked by a commune of the people, taken prisoner with his wife and children and placed in the Temple, while the people of Paris ran riot.

That was the year that the guillotine made its first appearance in the Place de la Grève in front of the Hôtel de Ville. It was later moved to the Place de la Revolution (now Place de la Concorde) and there, on January 21st, 1793, Louis XVI of France lost his life.

From that time the floodgates were opened and there seemed no finer thing than killing royalists. Through the streets of Paris rumbled the Terror with its carts full of the condemned, food for Madame la Guillotine, her appetite insatiable, hour after hour, day after day. In the 13 months before June 1794 there were 1,220 executions; in the seven weeks thereafter 1,376. From first to last there were condemned and executed some 4,000 people and it is no exaggeration to say that the streets of the city ran red and that in that 'Reign of Terror' looting and killing were the law.

Left: The Arc du Carousel. Outside the Louvre at the beginning of the Tuileries, this magnificent triumphal arch was built to celebrate Napoleon's victories of 1805.
Below: Commanding the Place Charles de Gaulle, the 165 feet high Arc de Triomphe is one of the most glorious of Paris monuments – and one of the great landmarks of the city.

Revolution is no builder and it was not until internal peace had been secured that Paris and her inhabitants were able to set to work and restore her beauty.

With Napoleon the city continued its evolution. And his love of splendour, of the Egyptian and Greco-Roman styles, left an indelible mark. Bonaparte lived in state in the Tuileries and during his time Paris was constantly enriched: The Arc de Triomphe was begun, the Arc du Carrousel in the Louvre completed. And so too was the church of the Madeleine—as a temple of glory. The Rue de Rivoli with its arcades was built and in the Place Vendôme a great column erected—to Napoleon himself. The Bourse (stock exchange) was constructed, also in temple fashion and the Louvre was enlarged. But Napoleon was a man of the future as well as the past and in his time the first iron bridges of the Pont des Arts and Pont d'Austerlitz appeared—as well as large cemeteries outside the busy quarters of the city, for the many dead of the new regime.

The defeat of Napoleon led to the reinstatement of the Bourbon dynasty in the person of the ineffectual Louis XVIII. He was succeeded by Charles X, but the people of Paris were conscious now of their power and when Charles started to muzzle the press they rose. And during the three glorious days of July 27-29th, 1830, students and workers, fighting side by side on the barricades, overthrew the Bourbon dynasty.

In its place they installed Louis Phillipe, but after 18 years overthrew him in turn in the February revolution of 1848. Here, once again, the people of Paris spontaneously constituted themselves as a sovereign body and took up the reins of power. The Second Republic was not destined to last long, however, and in October 1850 Louis Napoleon Bonaparte, nephew of the Emperor, secured his election as President of France—taking an oath to the democratic ideal and to regard as enemies all who attempted to change that form of government. Two years later he was emperor of France.

The reign of Napoleon III (1852-1870), even though its end saw the seige, bombardment and occupation of Paris by the Prussians, was a period of extraordinary splendour for the city.

Up to this time Paris, despite its grandeur, was in many ways still a medieval city. But now, with the aid of his prefect Baron Haussman, Napoleon quite literally took large portions of it apart—to recreate them in an image that was modern and new.

To build strategic highways and construct buildings according to Paris's economic need, Haussmann gutted the old city—paying particular attention to those poorer quarters that had in the past bred revolution. The mass of slums and small houses on the Ile de la Cité was demolished. Broad straight streets were cut through slum districts on each bank. Railway stations were built and large rectilinear streets designed around them. In the centre the Boulevards Saint Michel, Sébastopol and Strasbourg; in the west a system of avenues radiated from the Étoile and in the east from the Place de la Nation. The Latin Quarter was pierced by such streets as Saint Germain. The Opéra dates from this period and around the city a series of public parks was formed including the Bois de Vincennes and Bois de Boulogne. Not only this, the Louvre was once again extended and completed in a style to match the existing buildings—and beneath the streets an extensive sewage system built.

In short, a new and finer Paris appeared: more open, regular, comfortable, better lit and policed. By 1870, with a population approaching two million, Paris was the most beautiful and active city in Europe.

The Second Empire crumbled in the quick defeat of the Franco-Prussian War. Outraged at the news of Napoleon's surrender at Sedan (Sept 4th, 1870), the people of Paris decided to fight on alone. And for four months they managed to hold out against the entire strength of the German army who laid seige to the city. But famine finally forced its surrender. A brief occupation by the Prussians followed and then, when Napoleon had abdicated, France elected a new government— that of the Third Republic.

But the Parisians would have nothing to do with it. Independent as ever, they established a revolutionary junta—the Paris Commune. And for three months this body was to rule the city. Then the government forces advanced from Versailles.

Heavy streetfighting followed and, one by one, the barricades were overcome. But as the Communards retreated, they destroyed. They overthrew the Colonne Vendôme. They set fire to the centre of the city from the Tuileries to the Hôtel de Ville, including a good part of the

L'Opera, surely the largest and most lavish operatic theatre in the world. It was founded in 1669 and is now owned by the State.

Faubourg Saint Germain. Over 220 buildings were destroyed, among them the Tuileries Palace (which was never rebuilt) and the Hôtel de Ville, which was.

Finally cornered in the Cemetery of Père Lachaise, the Communards made their last stand where the small and tightly packed stone oratories provided some protection—though not enough. For at the end of a day's fighting 147 of them were captured, lined up against the cemetery wall and shot.

Meanwhile, the Third Republic set about making good the damage, and, in an attempt to restore Paris in world opinion, began to hold great exhibitions. To these are due the Trocadero (1878), the Eiffel Tower (1889) and the Grand Palais and Petit Palais (1900). At the turn of the century too, the great underground railway, the Métro was begun. Not long after that, Paris was once again at war.

In 1914 the German Army reached the Marne River, only a few miles from the capital. The French defended it desperately. For four days more than a million men were locked in mortal combat. As the battle came to a climax, General Gallieni, commander of the city, ordered that every taxi driver take fresh troops to the front. They did. Their action tipped the balance—and Paris was saved. And though it was later shelled by the great gun the Parisians nicknamed 'Big Bertha', the Germans never reached the city.

The post-war period that followed was a troubled one and gave small loveliness to the city. In 1919 the demolition of fortifications had begun and in their place rose rank upon rank of apartment buildings. The suburbs extended in tangles. All over Paris buildings were built of brick or cement, replacing—and much less beautiful than—those previously built in stone. Only one great work of this period can rival anything built before—the splendid Palais de Chaillot (1937). A mere four years later the Germans were occupying the city.

Although it must seem small comfort to those who endured the years of the cold and hunger of that occupation, and to the thousands of Parisians deported and killed, the judgement of history may yet conclude that occupation was a blessing in disguise. For by it the city was preserved from the devastation of modern warfare. And, above all, the bombing that in other capitals destroyed forever so much that was fine of the past.

After the war, Paris quickly resumed its rightful place in the world. Twice she has hosted the General Assembly of the United Nations and has been the seat of such well-known international organizations as NATO and UNESCO.

Although, in central Paris, little new was done in the way of building since the war, in the 1960s under Malraux's Ministry for Fine Arts, a great work of cleaning and beautifying was undertaken. Ancient monuments like the Louvre, L'Opéra and Nôtre Dame now glow with a honey-coloured freshness that belies their great antiquity. More recently too, ultra-modern works like the Tour Montparnasse and the futuristic developments of La Défense have altered the skyline. They show Paris on the move again: a great capital taking a lead once more into the architecture of the future.

This then is the background of Paris. A vital facet in an understanding of the city, for it explains much of the character, the quality, of the place, not just in terms of monuments, but of spirit.

It is a spirit that is piquant, sharp, indomitable. In the last 125 years Paris has known three revolutions, the armies of the Cossacks, the Prussians and of Adolf Hitler camped on the Champs Elysées. Now they are all gone and Paris remains, like the symbol of the eternal flame that burns below the Arc de Triomphe—victorious.

It is a fitting symbol for this city which has shrugged off conquerors, come through so much, yet retained its beauty and its character: rebellious, original, undefeated.

Some things in Paris never change – one of the city's most common sights, a woman shaking sheets from a window.

Above: Old comes down to make way for the new in the ever-evolving city. This particular demolition is in Montparnasse.

Paris of the Past

Every stone in Paris is steeped in the past and the events of her long and mighty history speak out on every boulevard and street corner, through a column, a monument or an arch.

The 17th–century Porte-Saint-Denis, for example, tells of the victories of Louis XIV, who in less than two months conquered more than 40 German strongholds. Napoleon's Vendôme column has its bas-relief cast from the 1,200 cannon the Emperor captured at Austerlitz. The 3000-year-old Obelisk of Luxor in the Place de la Concorde, brought from Egypt by Louis Philippe, stands where the guillotine once stood. And the mighty, soulless mausoleum of the Panthéon is built on the site of a medieval convent – itself occupying ground where there was once a Roman temple to Diana.

Paris is a city of visible, living antiquity. And of all Paris perhaps no building is more representative than the incredible Palais du Louvre.

One of the world's greatest palaces, larger even than the Vatican, the history of the Louvre traces that of the city itself. The very name probable comes from the Saxon *Leovar,* meaning a fortified dwelling. And this is how it started: as a feudal fortress outside the island city in the year 1200. From that time on, like Paris, it grew out in strength and beauty and the massive, two-pronged-fork-shaped complex of buildings one sees today is the result of the work of 17 kings over some 700 years.

In the 14th century Charles the Wise enlarged the fortress; in the 16th, Francois I made it his official residence – and demolished the fortifications, replacing them with a Renaissance-style palace. In their turn, Henri II and Catherine de Medicis constructed the Tuileries Palace and united it with the existing structures. In 1682, however, the court was transferred to Versailles. And gradually the Louvre ran down. Little by little, squatters moved in and by 1750 the palace had fallen into such disrepair that its demolition was considered. But then came Napoleon, ejecting the squatters, restoring splendour; and clearing the slums around the palace. His nephew Napoleon III completed his work. Which left the palace as it is today? Not quite. For in 1870 the Communards burnt down the Tuileries Palace, thus opening out the western side of the Louvre to the long, lovely vistas over the Tuileries gardens and Place de la Concorde.

Nor is the Louvre any longer a royal palace – though never has it held more wealth. Today it is one of the largest, most richly endowed museums in the world, containing some of the most highly prized of paintings and sculptures – not least among which are the *Venus de Milo* and the *Mona Lisa.*

In a way the Louvre defines the very quality of historical Paris. For, despite its long and varied history and the different centuries that have made their contribution to its constuction, there is a sense of unity about it. It seems to come together as a whole. Like Paris herself, an integral and living entity.

The once notorious Palais de Justice. In its huge complex of buildings is the Conciergerie where Queen Marie-Antoinette awaited execution.

Left: Statue of Charlemagne, the great Frankish emperor, beside Nôtre-Dame. He died in 814.
Right: The 169 feet high July Column in the Place de la Bastille. It stands on the site of the terrible Bastille prison, which the people of Paris pulled down in 1789. The column itself was erected in memory of those who died in the risings of 1830 and 1848.

Left: The elegance of the Marais, a district reclaimed from swampland.
Right: The Institute of France. It was designed by the renowned architect Le Vau and built in the mid-17th century as the result of a legacy from Cardinal Mazarin.
Below: At any moment in the streets of Paris you may encounter splendour such as this.

Above: The tomb of the Unknown Soldier with its eternal flame, below the Arc de Triomphe.

Above Right: A street of the Latin Quarter – a very old part of Paris and a scholastic centre since the 13th century.

City of Churches

Paris has been a Christian city for 1500 years and of all its myriad wonders few surpass the churches. Their variety is amazing, spanning the centuries in every conceivable style and position, nestling into the surrounding architecture or standing clear—each one a unique and beautiful jewel.

Of all the great churches of Paris, Nôtre Dame, one of the oldest , is surely the most beautiful. The first of the French gothic churches, begun in 1163 on the Ile de la Cité on the site of a Roman Temple, it is constructed in the shape of a Latin cross: 427 feet long, 164 feet wide and 130 feet high. An incredible structure for the 12th century, it took more than 100 years to complete. Over the ages since, its vast weight has caused it to sink more than three feet.

Almost as well-known, though very much newer, the white-stone basilica of the Sacré-Coeur stands, commanding the hill of Montmartre, one of the great landmarks of Paris. Begun in 1876 and consecrated in 1919, it was constructed as the result of a national subscription, to which three million Frenchmen contributed. A curious mixture of Byzantine and Romanesque styles, the church is 328 feet long, 164 feet wide and 308 feet high. Its bell, the 'Savoyarde', at more than 20 tons, is one of the largest in the world.

In total contrast is Saint-Germain-des-Prés, near the heart of the Latin Quarter, the oldest church in Paris. A fine example of Romanesque architecture, it was originally a monastic chapel of the sixth century. Destroyed more than once by the Normans, it was finally rebuilt in the 11th century. At the time of the Revolution it was used as a saltpetre store. Today St Germain holds the tomb of the great philosopher Descartes.

Far grander is the Madeleine: superbly positioned at the end of the Rue Royale, facing the Place de la Concorde. Designed along Grecian lines, it was built by Napoleon as a temple of glory for the soldiers of his 'Grande Armee' and has neither transept nor side aisles. After Bonaparte's fall, it was considered for several uses — including a railway station — before finally being consecrated a church. With a colonnade of 52 Corinthian columns 65 feet high, the Madeleine is of magnificent proportions: 355 feet long, 141 wide and 98 high.

Built in the 12th century on the site of a sixth century building, the gothic church of Saint-Germain-L'Auxerrois is uniquely famous. For this was the church that signalled the Saint Bartholomew's Day Massacre of Protestants on August 24th 1572. Today, however, its 44 glorious bells play a different tune and the church's interior is a wealth of art and stone carvings and glass from the 15th century. Right outside the Louvre, it was virtually a royal chapel and here were buried royal jesters and many of the artists patronized by the Crown.

Sacré-Coeur by night. The great white dome is visible from almost every part of Paris and dominates Montmartre at its feet.

Above Left: Reflections of a city of
churches.
Left: The cemetery of Montmartre,
where many famous men are buried,
including Zola, Degas and Stendhal.
Right: The Mosque – an unexpected
corner of the orient in the heart of
medieval Paris.

Left: Nôtre-Dame's 12th century door of Saint Anne.
Right: Viollet le Duc's 19th century gargoyles on Nôtre-Dame.
Below: Nôtre-Dame from the Seine. The great church took more than 100 years to build. It was restored in the 19th century when the central spire was added.

Gay Paree

Announce that you're off to Paris for the weekend, and people may well smile knowingly. How wrong they would be!

Paris has long had the reputation of being a 'naughty' city: it dates from the 1890s, the time of the can-can, and was confirmed in the 1930s and 1950s, when the city offered ladies shedding clothes with more abandon then anywhere else in Europe. But, alas, standards change – and Paris deserves its reputation no more.

True, the floorshow at the Lido is sumptuously staged; they still do the can-can at the Moulin Rouge; and the Folies Bergères has the longest legs (many of them English) you're ever likely to see. True, the girls at the Crazy Horse Saloon are stunning and disrobe with consummate artistry – but what are these things to the late 1970s? Certainly not 'naughty'. Indeed, in comparison with, say, Amsterdam, Stockholm – or even London – Paris today is decidedly sedate!

And yet – few cities have such an atmosphere of zest, verve, *joie de vivre*. Paris is a living testament to the fact that the French enjoy life – that they respect the right of others to, however individually – and have made of living an art.

The city never stops, never closes. There are 51 theatres, numerous cinemas, cafés, bars, the most glamorous shops, more than 6,000 restaurants. Somewhere or other, one of these is always open and, at any time of the day or night, you can enjoy a drink or meal – and what a meal that will be!

At the famous Maxim's in the Rue Royale, for instance, you will find unsurpassed food in surroundings of an elegance that has not changed since the *Belle Epoch* of the 1890s. In total contrast, the equally famous La Coupôle in Montparnasse, a railway-station-sized restaurant crammed with writers and painters and 'types', will serve you a superb and reasonably-priced meal into the early hours – if you can find a seat!

But perhaps one of the greatest charms of *'Gay Paree'* is its sidewalk cafés. They line the great boulevards; they dot the squares; you find them everywhere – and it is here that the French themselves spend so much of their time: discussing, dreaming and regarding others regarding them. Here you can enjoy at one and the same time the sights of the city and its life. Sip a *petit blanc sec* (dry white wine) or *café arrosé* (coffee with a spot of brandy) and in just a little time you will see the world go by. Indeed, in this mood much of Parisian political, cultural and artistic life has been engendered at its cafés. Those like the *Deux Magots* (magot means grotesque Chinese figure!) have long been a meeting place for philosophers, artists and writers. Even more renowned perhaps, and certainly more elegant, is the *Café de la Paix* on the corner of the Place de l'Opéra – the great original which has provided the name and model for cafés throughout the French-speaking world.

Action at the Crazy Horse Saloon! Founded in 1951 it is the city's best-known night-spot and a must for broad-minded visitors.

Left: The 19th century Moulin Rouge, where the can-can was born.
Below: A typically Parisian sidewalk cafe. The city is full of such places.

Right: The famous Left Bank cafe and meeting place *Aux Deux Magots.* Situated on The Boulevard St Germain, the cafe takes its name from the sign of a chinese silk screen shop which once stood here.
Below: There is always a restaurant or cafe open somewhere in Paris – 24 hours a day.

Left: The renowned Maxim's restaurant in the Rue Royale is the well-heeled gourmet's paradise.
Below Left: Paris is a city of individuals.
Above: French humour: the depressed-looking figure here is saying, 'I'm very funny'.
Right: The Parisians love to discuss life. These two old women are outside a famous fish restaurant. The bin on which one of them sits on is full of shell-fish shells.

Paris Markets

The greatest of all Paris markets was Les Halles, originating in the 12th century, described by Zola as 'the belly of Paris' and in its heyday occupying, in covered area alone, ten acres. Today, it has gone, a victim of modernization, but Paris remains no less a thriving and ebullient trading city, with a multitude of street markets and shops — deep in cellars, in the underground, up twisting stairs, in restaurants — in the most unexpected places!

Starting at the top, in the 1st and 2nd *arrondisements* (Paris is divided into 20 of these administrative zones) you will find a quartier *luxe.* Consisting of the Rue de la Paix, de Castiglione, Saint Honoré, the Place Vendôme and the Rue de Rivoli, this is an area of supreme elegance — probably containing the finest jewellery and luxury items in the world.

At the other extreme, on the quays of the Seine and especially on the Left Bank round the Ile de la Cité, are the famous Parisian *bouquinistes.* With their large wooden book cases perched on the parapets over the river banks, each of them sells very similar-looking, second-hand books and prints.

Across the river on the Ile de la Cité is the Place Louis-Lepine, site of the Marché aux Fleurs. This is the magnificent Paris flower market. And every day of spring and summer it intoxicatingly assaults the senses with hundreds of different scents and blooms. Every day, that is, except Sundays. For then the flower market is given over to birds.

The Marché aux Oiseaux is an upsetting sight, but nonetheless an extraordinary one: for the Place Louis Lepine is filled with hundreds upon thousands of caged birds. (Far too many to a cage sometimes.) They are of every type from canaries to pheasants and of every conceivable colour. Some are even dyed!

Perhaps the most renowned of all Paris markets is the Marché aux Puces, the flea market, at Clignancourt. Here, on Saturday, Sunday and Monday, you can see just about everything imaginable in the way of second-hand goods. Spilling over the pavements, the place has immense 'colour'. Anyone who can find space and the fee can sell here. The vendors range from tramps with rubbish-dump junk, to polished professionals. It's said you can't find a bargain in the flea market, but it has been done and the thing to remember is – haggle!

As well as this, Paris has a Dog and Donkey Market; a Stamp Market; a Wine Market; a Gingerbread Fair and a Ham Fair (which also features scrap iron!). Indeed, in a sense, the city herself is one great market, for each district has at least one weekly market day and everywhere, clothing, food, flowers, and bon-bons are temptingly displayed.

The shop windows of Paris are a minor art form in themselves. The simplest *boulangerie* calls with its fresh-bake smell and appetising stacks of long loaves. And even at the most modest *boucherie* you are quite likely to see an entire pig's head — with a flower in its mouth!

A Paris street market. This one is in Montparnasse, and is typical of many throughout the city.

Above: Marché aux Puces, the most famous of all Paris markets, the Flea Market at Clignancourt.
Right: Bouquinists by the Seine. And just across the river, the stately pile of Nôtre-Dame.

Left: The Marché aux Oiseaux in the Place Louis-Lépine. This notorious bird market sells every imaginable kind of bird as pets or for the pot!
Above Left: A butcher and his assistant contemplate his handiwork.
Above: Part of the beautiful Marché aux Fleurs, or flower market, on the Ile de la Cité. On Sunday the flowers give way to the birds.

Two sides of Paris fashion:
Below: The vast selection of ready-
to-wear clothes in a Paris store.
Below Right: A mannequin displays
a couturier's collection at one of the
city's innumerable fashion shows.

Cultural Paris

A harmony of old and new, of function and design, a city where on any street corner you may encounter a minor masterpiece, Paris is itself a living work of art.

From the statues of the Tuileries to the triumphs of the Musée Rodin; from the pavement artists of Montmartre to the Leonardos of the Louvre; from the Left Bank *bavardiers* to the masters of the Comédie Francaise, Paris's cultural life is unbelievably rich. And as French culture finds its quintessence in the visual and dramatic arts, it is only fitting that, in this her prime city and its environs, there should be no less than 51 theatres and 107 museums.

Indisputedly foremost among these is the Louvre. Repository of works of art from ancient Egypt and the Orient and Greece and Rome, through medieval right up to modern times, this one museum holds 400,000 treasures in all.

Then? Everyone will have their preference. The Musée du Jeu de Paume in the Place de la Concorde has a staggering collection of Impressionists; among them, Manet, Monet, van Gogh, Renoir, Degas, Cezanne — many of whom of course lived in Paris. Other museums not be missed are the Carnavalet; the Musée de Cluny; the Palais de l'Alma and the Musée Rodin. Les Invalides, where Napoleon is buried is also a museum of armour and regimental relics. The Palais de Chaillot which was built for the exhibition of 1937, also houses the Musée de l'Homme.

From the time of Napoleon III one of the great cultural centres of Paris has been the Opéra. The largest theatre for opera in the world (covering an area of 120,000 square feet) it is a spectacle in itself: even more ornate inside than out, with its sumptuous, onyx-balustraded grand staircases, multi-coloured marble foyers, magnificent chandeliers and, since 1966, a fresco by Chagall.

No look at cultural Paris would be complete, though, without a mention of the Comédie Francaise. The most important of the five Paris theatres subsidized by the State, in its foyer one can see the statues of the great dramatic writers: Voltaire, Molière, Victor Hugo, Dumas and many others. Here at reasonable prices one can 'assist' at the great classics of French theatre, the works of Molière, Racine and Corneille. Here too are performed the great moderns such as Claudel and Anouilh. But as well as all this, the Comédie Francaise has an extra importance in French culture. For more than any other institution, it enshrines ideals that are integral to French civilization, the classical ideals of patriotism, courage, courtesty, virtues of living and of language that the French esteem.

The glorious Chagall ceiling at the Opéra, the Paris home of State-subsidized opera and ballet.

Left: Just part of the vast architectural complex of the Louvre, the city's most important museum and art gallery.
Below Right: Le Penseur or *the Thinker* by Rodin, France's best-known sculptor.
Below Left: The École Militaire – the military academy – at the end of the Champs de Mars, where Napoleon studied.

Right: A portrait of Racine, the 17th century poet and dramatist, at the Comédie Francaise.
Below: The exterior of the Comédie Francaise, formed in 1680.
Far Right: A typically Parisian apartment building of the 15th *arrondisement*.

Parks and Gardens

Paris does not have a large, centrally situated park, such as Hyde Park in London or Central Park in New York. In terms of green metres per capita, it offers less than many other capitals. Yet, wandering down its chestnut-lined streets, there is no sense of this; strolling through its glorious gardens one is amazed to find such ordered beauty and tranquility in a city. In Paris' two great parks with their lakes and woodlands, there is a feeling of being in the countryside itself.

Most used by Parisians and probably most loved of her gardens is the Jardin de Luxembourg. Elegantly stretching away in front of the Palace of Luxembourg, it extends for 57 acres of lawns, terraces, trees, fountains, fine statues and even playing fields. A public park since the 17th century, it has long been a meeting-place for students from the nearby university and the serenity of its Medici fountain has proved the inspiration of countless writers and poets.

Next is the Jardin des Tuileries, a garden of order and elegance, covering half a mile betwen the Place de la Concorde and the Place de la Carrousel, outside the Louvre. Superbly laid out in the later half of the 17th century by Le Nôtre, it consists of long sides with high, tree-planted terraces, flanking a wide central area of lawns, chestnuts,

limes and beautiful geometric flower beds. There are ponds (with trout!) a shaded children's playground, and statues absolutely everywhere: by Cosysevox, Coustou, Pradier, Le Poultre.

On the east of the city is its great park – the Bois de Vincennes. At 2,308 acres, this is the largest park in Paris. A private park since the 13th century, it was given to the people by Napoleon III and today contains the zoo – one of the finest in Europe – and several museums, woods, three lakes with islands, an Indochinese temple, a tropical garden and a floral park, displaying hundreds of different types of flowers.

More elegant than Vincennes and almost opposite on the west of Paris, is the Bois de Boulogne. Until 1852 it was part of a forest with several châteaux. In that year, though, it was given to the city by Napoleon III, who commissioned Haussmann to replan it. The wood became a vast park, inspired, it is said, by Hyde Park.

Today, with its woods and lawns and waterfalls and gardens, the Bois de Boulogne covers an area of more than 2,200 acres. The park is a favourite recreational area for Parisians, with boating on the larger of its two artificial lakes, a zoo in the Jardin d'Acclimation, horse-riding in the woods and two racecourses, the famous Longchamps and Auteuil.

Just one of the scores of glorious statues throughout the Tuileries. The gardens were laid out in the 18th century.

Below: This avenue in the '15th' is typical of the charm of so much of the city.
Right: The ubiquitous game of boule – played here in the Luxembourg gardens.
Bottom Right: The Jardins du Luxembourg, leading down to the Luxembourg palace, built in 1615 by Marie de Medici, wife of Henri IV.

Left: The famous Medici Fountain by
Salomon de Brosse.
Below: Statue of student resistance
in the Luxembourg Gardens.

AMI SI TV TOMBEL VN AMI SORT DE L'OMBRE A TA PLACE

AVX ETVDIANTS RESISTANTS

Left: The fountain of the four corners of the world in the Jardins du Luxembourg.
Below: The early 17th century Place des Vosges is perfectly square – 354 feet long on every side – and encompassed by picturesque mansions. It is the city's oldest square.

Modern Paris

Paris quite possibly contains and consists of a greater multitude of treasures of art and architecture than any other city. For this reason, it has been likened to one vast museum; but the comparison is invalid. For Paris is a living entity – and as such is constantly evolving. In the process a new Paris rises round the old, evoking the criticism of traditionalists for its striking modernity, yet incorporating architecture of superb design, as advanced and beautiful as any in the world.

Built for the Exhibition of 1889, the Eiffel Tower began modern Paris and in its way has still not been equalled. Some 984 feet high (except in warm weather when it can rise up to eight inches) it is composed of 12,000 metal parts fastened by two and a half million rivets. Yet it weighs only 7,000 tons and with its four 'feet' covering an area of more than two acres, is calculated to exert no greater pressure on the earth per square inch than a man does seated in a chair.

There are three floors: the first at 190 feet; the second at 380; and the third at 905. This top floor provides an unrivalled view of all Paris. On a clear day the view carries as far as 40 miles.

Much more recent, and in their way quite as striking, are the high-rise futuristic buildings erected in the 1960s and 1970s in the Quartier de la Defénse. Most notable feature among these is the vast hall of the Centre National des Industries et des Techniques, for its extraordinary swooping vault covers an area of no less than 980,000 square feet, with only three points of support.

The airport of Charles de Gaulle deserves mention, too, as the most modern in Western Europe. A triumph of logical design, it incorporates a central body, from which radiate octopoidal arms. Served by moving walkways, each of these ends in a 'satellite' hub, with which the appropriate airplane is able to make direct contact.

The massively functional high-rise housing development around the Gare Montparnasse is something of a bugbear for the critics of modern Paris. They might well have a point—were it not for the grace of the Tour Montparnasse, which soars above it all, lifting the entire complex. A slender and elegant 58 storey building, (with at its summit the most scenic restaurant in Europe, the Tour Montparnasse has, since the 1970s, become a feature of the Paris skyline, loved by some Parisians, grunted at by others. It is undeniably impressive by day and by night dramatic, seeming to glow black against the sky, with a darkness that is only intensified by the horizontal strips of red light set at intervals along its great sides.

The most recent arrival on the Paris scene and completed in 1976, is the controversial Beaubourg. Erected on the site of part of the ancient market of Les Halles as a museum for modern art and culture, it is a vast, box-shaped, steel and concrete structure with convertible floor space, served by enclosed and moving walkways outside the building. From a distance they have the appearance of huge coloured tubes.

Third floor roof garden by the Sheraton Hotel in Montparnasse. In the foreground a pedestrian walkway crosses high above the Rue René Mouchotte.

Left: The Palais de Chaillot (1937), as seen from the first floor of the Eiffel Tower. It houses an underground theatre and various museums.
Below: Most famous of all the landmarks of this great city – the Eiffel Tower. Built in 1889, it soars 984 feet above Paris.

Below Left: 19th century
appartment building in
Montparnasse.
Right: Changing the skyline:
construction in the 15th
arrondissement.
Below Right: The Pompidou Centre
in the Beaubourg.

Along the Seine

Paris began on the Ile de la Cité in the River Seine. It is the river to day, as it has always been, which provides the city with so much of its character and grace.

More central to Paris then the Thames is to London, or the Tiber is to Rome (and probably more beautiful and atmospheric than both) the Seine flows clean through the city in a long majestic loop for some eight miles and divides it into two almost equal parts, the Rive Droite (Right Bank) and the Rive Gauche (Left Bank).

Very much an inland river, too far from the sea for any tang of salt or cry of seagull, the Seine is slow-flowing and at Paris only about 100 feet above sea-level. Throughout the centuries it has become controlled by man and is very much a tamed river now, little wider than the great Parisian avenues and dredged as far as Rouen to a constant depth of 10 feet. Walled in along its length by stone quays, frequently lined with trees, the river is crossed in Paris by no less than 33 bridges, the oldest being the Pont Neuf (meaning 'New Bridge'), which was begun in 1578.

With its two tributaries, the Marne and the Oise, the Seine has to drain the whole of the low-lying plain of Northern France, and however tamed it may be, still has its angry moods. In the past it used to rise to flood tide and in 1448 and 1590, when it was almost possible to cross the summer river on foot, winter saw terrible floods that wrought havoc in the city. Even as recently as 1910, the water level rose an astonishing eight metres and the city was flooded as far as the Gare St Lazare. Parisians mark the rise of the river by its relationship to the Zouave soldier at the foot of the Pont D'Alma. At the height of the 1910 flood he was standing in water up to his neck!

The borders of the Seine provide some of the loveliest views in all Paris: changing, colourful, panoramic. On the Right Bank, the Quai de la Rapée is lined with great trees that shade calm alleys. Further west, over the ancient stones of the Pont Marie, is the haven of 17th century houses on the Ile Saint-Louis. And downstream, at the furthest point of the boat-shaped Ile de la Cité, there is the sense that it is almost the island which moves, not the river. Further downstream the quays are lined with *bouquinistes* and extend to the Carrousel and Les Invalides. Upstream, between the Pont d'Arcole and the Pont d'Austerlitz, is the commercial Port of Paris and to this, through a network of river and canals, come goods from all over France.

Parisians have always made the most of the Seine. Along its banks they sit, stroll and meditate. Lovers find an idyllic rendezvous, fishermen idle away the hours (and sometimes even catch a perch or two) and the famous Parisian *clochards* (tramps) find a resting place beneath the bridges. Constantly changing, bringing a band of sky to the earth and everywhere spreading varying shades of light, the Seine reflects the great city that it refreshes and renews. It is the balm and one of the great joys of Paris.

The Ile de la Cité – where Paris
began around 2000 years ago.

Right: Fishermen at the Quai de La Megisserie.
Below: Nôtre-Dame seen from across the river.
Below Right: A *clochard,* or tramp, finds a little comfort on the Right Bank of the Seine.

Below: The Pont Neuf, built between 1578 and 1606 and the oldest of the city's 33 bridges.
Below Right: On the Left Bank, a painter finds his inspiration by the river.

Left: 'Down by the bridges of
Paris . . .'
Above: The Ile de la Cité as seen
from Ile St Louis.
Right: On the furthermost point of
the Ile de la Cité, a man meditates by
the calm waters of the Seine.

Paris Underground

The wonders of Paris do not end with her streets or the Seine, but continue way beneath both.

When Haussmann first built the sewers of Paris in the Reign of Napoleon III, they were considered one of the triumphs of the emerging city. They are still of interest today. A virtual city underground, the sewers cover no less than 12,600 acres and carry, as well, water, gas and electricity mains, telegraph and telephone. From their inception they have exerted a fascination. The writer, Victor Hugo immortalised them in *Les Misérables;* they were one of the most fashionable of tourist attractions at the turn of the century (along with the morgue); and even now, in the season, conducted tours leave from the Place de la Concorde four times a week.

In their grim fashion, the Paris *catacombes* are of even greater interest than the sewers. They extend under the Left Bank from the Place Denfert-Rôchereau all the way to the Jardin des Plantes, a honeycomb of ancient quarries some 60 feet below the surface, the result of stone mining that was going on as far back as Roman times.

When the Cîmetière des Innocents was demolished in 1786, the bones were disinterred and brought to the *catacombes* in carts. At first this was done reverently, but as numbers grew and the contents of still further cemeteries were added, the reverence faded. In the end the grisly remains were treated as just so much rubbish to be dumped. And so it was—in these tunnels and quarries—all that remained of three million people.

In the 19th century, someone with a grim sense of order had the bones rearranged: in patterns of skulls, rib-cages, etc. and the *catacombes* today consist of a labyrinth of galleries lined with bones and skulls. It was in this setting in the last war that the opposition to the Germans had its headquarters in August of 1944. And here too that those Communards who escaped the massacre at Père Lachaise were finally caught by government troops—and slaughtered among the skeletons.

A far more cheerful side of Paris, without which no book on the city would be complete, is the Métro: the city's underground railway, which is often overground too! One of the most efficient, and surely the most attractive, systems of its kind in the world, the Métro provides the fastest, cheapest and least strenuous way of getting round the city. A train arrives approximately every two minutes. Many of the trains are quite silent, running on rubber wheels. The whole thing has been thought through with typical French logic: the same fare takes you to any station (though you can travel first or second class). And, as it's impossible to get in without paying, you don't lose time bothering to surrender your ticket on the way out.

As much as anything in Paris their subway exemplifies the French love of beauty. For the stations are not merely clean; each is distinctive, light, individually decorated. Many are downright attractive and stations such as Louvre, for instance, even exhibit antiquities and

The Louvre station in the Métro: so lavish, one feels the train has actually arrived inside the museum itself.

works of art such as you find in the museum itself.

The Métro exemplifies much of what Paris is about: efficient and moving with the times, but with a dogged individualism that is not prepared to surrender beauty to expedience. It is a trait that, running throughout her history, has made Paris what she is today: beautiful, unique—one of the great cities of the world.

Left: The station at La Defénse.
Below: A typical art nouveau entrance to the Métro.

Below Left: One of the more bizarre of Paris tourist attractions, the sewers.
Right: Some of the machinery that keeps it all going.
Below Right: The *Catacombes* – once the macabre repository of some three million skeletons.

Taking a Trip

Paris is a superbly compact city which, with a little help from the Métro, can be comfortably covered on foot. And she is equally well-placed for outings. For the countryside is quickly reached and of all the many excursions one can enjoy, none requires travelling more than 15 miles from the centre of the city.

The flea market at Clignancourt, the park of Vincennes, the Bois de Boulogne, all are easily accessible – and even racing at Longchamps, you are still within sight of the Eiffel Tower. So are you too at the park of Saint-Cloud, a favourite resort of Parisians. Once containing an old château which was burnt down by the Prussians, a fountain and terrace remain and from here the view is magnificent: with the Tour d'Eiffel seeming to rise from the very trees of the Bois de Boulogne.

Other parks worth visiting, too, are: the Parc des Buttes, Chaumont, with its artificial waterfall and high island crowned by a Greek temple; and the Jardin des Plantes – which features a botanical gardens, a maze and zoo.

Not far from the Jardin des Plantes is the Arènes de Lutèce, the remains of a Roman arena. Not a great deal is left, but you can still see the names of spectators carved in the stone of the benches. Today the arena itself, where once Christians were martyred, is a favourite place for the omni-popular French game of boules.

But most gratifying of all the excursions from Paris is Versailles. One of the wonders of France, a quarter-mile long palace of pink and cream stone in the style of the classical period of the French Renaissance, Versailles has to be experienced to be believed. Originally a modest hunting-lodge, Louis XIV moved his court there from the Louvre, transforming it into a vast and splendid palace with heroic-sized statues and sumptuous state appartments. The finest of these, the Galerie des Glaces, is 240 feet long, 43 high, and has walls ornamented with green marble Corinthian pilasters and mirrors of Venetian glass. Created by Le Vau and Mansart and Le Brun, with its gardens exquisitely laid out by Le Nôtre, Versailles in its day accommodated in luxury Louis' household of no less than 20,000 people. With its vast size, lavish stuccos and frescoes and tapestries, it presents a vision of wealth and splendour that is quite staggering to the modern mind.

After such opulence, it is salutary to visit the cemetery of Père Lachaise. On the east of the city, this is the largest of Paris's cemeteries, the one to which the French themselves make pilgrimages, and which is literally crammed with the graves of the great. Oscar Wilde, Chopin, Molière, la Fontaine and many other famous men and women are all buried here. And the place presents as well one of the strangest sights of Paris. For it is packed with monuments, little oratories – row upon row of them – that look rather like stone telephone kiosks – and it was firing from these that the ill-fated communards made their famous and fatal last stand.

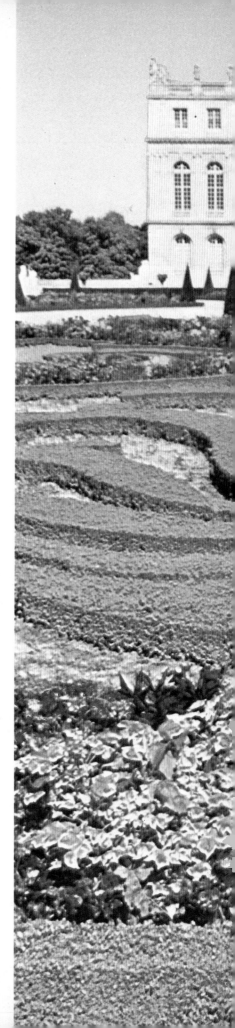

The beautiful gardens of Versailles. Designed by Le Nôtre in the 1660s, they cover, in all, an area of almost 250 acres.

Far Left: A fraction of the great exterior of the palace of Versailles.
Left: One of the scores of sumptuous state appartments inside the palace.
Below: Panoramic view from the palace terrace over the gardens.

Left: Boating in the Bois de Boulogne. Once a royal hunting park the area was given to Paris in 1852 by Napoleon III.
Below Left: With more than 2200 wooded acres, the Bois offers a wealth of places to picnic.
Below: These luxuriant woods are only minutes from central Paris.

Left: The racecourse at Longchamps, where one can lunch while watching the racing – with the finish directly below.
Below: The Eiffel Tower soaring above the Longchamps car park.

Below Left: The Parc des Buttes
Chaumont with its Greek temple.
Below: The grave of Edith Piaf,
France's famous singer who
became known as the 'little
sparrow'. She died in 1963.
Below Right: Oscar Wilde's grave in
Pere Làchaise cemetery, where so
many of the great are buried.